Why Spiders?

ELIZABETH EVANS BOOKS
© 2018 Carole Elizabeth Tomaszewicz
(Elizabeth Evans)

ISBN: 978-3-9525044-0-6 Paperback
EISBN: 978-3-9525044-1-3 E-Book

Elizabeth Evans Books
www.elizabethevans.simplesite.com
Zurich, Switzerland

Why Spiders? - First Edition, 2021

Additional Credit:
Illustrative Design & Page Layout - Elizabeth Evans, **Illustrations** - C.P. Milan, **Chief Editor** - Christine Evans, **Editing Support** - Kate Johnston, & Melody Thorpe, **Educational Consultancy** - Irena Tomaszewicz, Helena Tomaszewicz, & Julia Helling, **Tech Support** - Nahid Razon, **General Encouragement and Positive Vibes** - Alex Martin Evans & Sarah Lalaz

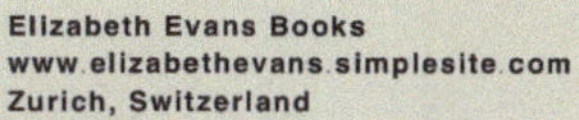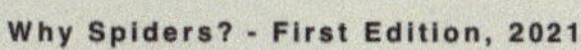

Have you ever wondered why
you're scared of certain things?

Like **slimy** slugs,

or **SUDDEN** sounds,

or tiny bats with wings?

Well, one thing I have thought about
and why it makes me nervous:

a **spider** living in my house –
what really is its purpose?

One day I looked upon a beast
sitting on its web,
in MY room, MY private space,
and this is what it said,

" HELLO, down there,
I'm watching you!
Don't think I just hear cries.
I can always see you with...

... my eight great blinking eyes!"

Round eyes, small eyes,
big eyes, Wink!
Shining, twinkling,
BLINK,
BLINK,
BLINK!

That great big spider spoke again while slowly moving nearer,
"I NEED my eyes to keep me safe and help me see things clearer."

So many eyes all looking down,
why wouldn't THAT be scary?

It's not got two, like me and you,
and it's also really...

...hairy!"

Long hair, SHORT HAIR,
STRAIGHT and curly,
Bouncing bunches,
Swirly-whirly.

That hairy spider spoke again
as it slowly moved my way,

"I need my hair to keep me safe,
and help me sense my prey."

One more thought then
came to mind,
how spiders make me worry:
the way they move
along the ground,
a creepy, silent...

...scurry!"
shhhh

Long legs,
Short legs,
scurrying fast!
Quickly, slowly,
SNEAKING PAST.

The spider took one giant leap
then crept up close to where I sleep.

It drew a breath
and calmly said,
"I'm sorry that I bring such DREAD.
My silent movements aren't for you,
they're simply what I need to do."

I'd had enOUGh
of explanation,
all this talk
and information.
So, letting it come closer still,
I reached up near my window sill,
"It's your turn now, your time is up!"
And...

...I quickly caught it in a cup!
Got it! Trapped it!
I felt relief,

that soon I'd suffer no more grief.
To my delight and satisfaction,
a plan was coming into ACTION!

I'd have no reason left to fear,
once this was far
away from here.

I knew deep down
it wasn't right,
but had to move it
from my sight!

Through the door and down the street,
I took it past the farm.
I didn't stop at the
ice cream shop
in case it caused alarm.

Across the stream and **further** still
until I reached the wood.
It **won't** find its way back again,
it's gone,
it's **out** for good!

I skipped with joy back on the path
So happy with my work.
That **beast** had left my private space,
no **longer** would it lurk.

But when I made it to my home
I truly understood,
why we have these spiders here
and how they do us good!
For when I opened up the door,
much to my surprise,
the house was
full up
to the brim with...

... loads of
BUZZING
flies!

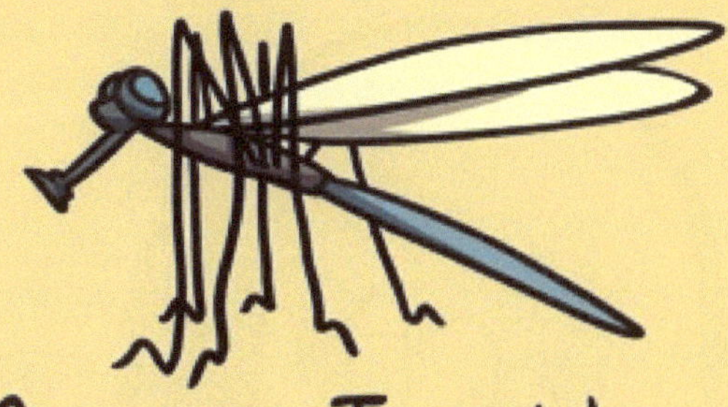

Some stinky, foul, and green!

Everywhere!

Some upside down!

And on the tv screen!

All those eyes to look around -
to search up HIGH and on the ground.

The **hairy legs** to sense each **rustle** -
of helpless flies caught in a tussle.

And creeping
round so silently -

It **needs** those flies to stay,
not flee!

So...now the flies were moving in,
no longer threatened by its grin.
I'd clearly made a HUGE mistake,
but quickly saw
what it would take,
to **rid** the filth, **the smell,
the flies!**
I'd finally opened up my eyes!

Back through the door and down the street
I SPRINTED past the farm,
then stopped to buy an ice cream
in the hope to keep it calm.

Across the stream and further still
until I reached the wood,
and begged it to come home again,
home again for good!

It took my gift of ice cream
and gave a little smile.
Being cast out in the forest
gave it chance to think a while.

So with one big lick,
and a crunch of cone
it then began to say,

"I'd **love** to come back home with you,
and there I'd like to stay.

There is just **one** condition though,"
the cunning spider said,
"I won't sleep on your ceiling now,
I much prefer your...

...bed!"